PELLiNORE

THE STORY OF A COTSWOLD CAT

BY

AURIEL FRÈRE

FIVE WRENS PRESS

INDEX OF CHAPTERS

THE PHOTOGRAPHS

The pictures in this book are some of the many taken of Pellinore, Scarlett and Sylvie by Malc and I over the years. They were un-posed, casual and quite spontaneous, but when I came to write the book we found we had so many different shots that a lot of the incidents I was writing about turned out to have photographic parallels.

Published by Five Wrens Press 2010.

ISBN: 978-0-9565413-0-7
Printed and bound in China by Toppan Printing Co. Ltd

"What is man without the beasts? If all the beasts were gone, man would die from a great loneliness of the spirit. For whatever happens to the beasts, soon happens to man. All things are connected."

From Chief Seattle's Oration, 1854.

PELLINORE

His paws were very soft and silky, the pads very dry – spongy yet sort of hard on top, except when he was stressed. Then they would feel like warm, slightly moist suede leather. He had silky pale ginger fur between his pink toes, which he kept scrupulously clean. When he had got mud or dirt on his soft, muscular paws, he would spread the toes and lick them clean, nuzzling at areas of intransigent dirt while making squeaky chomping noises, seizing any burrs between his teeth and spitting them contemptuously onto the carpet with a toss of his head. In summer one would find those burrs suddenly stuck to the soles of socks or edges of clothes if you knelt on the carpet.

The top of his head was also soft and silky. Its shape fitted closely into the palm of a cupped hand. He would often shake his head vigorously after, or during, the course of washing his ears with his paws. That gave rise to one of his many long-standing nicknames: "Old Flapperty Ears". His ears were very soft but sort of pert and flexible. If you fondled them they would yield easily to the touch but then spring back into their own perfect V-shape the next moment. They were like some kind of mystery substance that no matter how many times they were mauled about – in play, affection or in fights - they always sprang back unmarked, retaining a pristine sensitivity.

The fur on his ears lay very flat and gave the impression of being only one layer of hair deep. If you brushed your fingers against the flow of the grain it felt surprisingly sharp and prickly and resistant to the touch. The fur on his nose was rather similar, but if anything shorter and stiffer than the fur on his ears – it could not be touched in a way that altered its direction or flow. It ended in a horizontal line just above the un-furred part of his nose, which was either cold and wet to the touch, or warm and dry-feeling. He didn't like you to test the temperature of his nose and would always twist his head away if you tried to do it. The fur on his back and stomach was short, smooth and silky, plush and bushy in winter, less fluffy in summer when he was often afflicted with harvest mites that irritated his skin. The fur on his tummy was paler, softer and less banded with ginger than on his back and sides. Ginge's tail was in perfect proportion to the rest of him. It was long and full and elegant, with no kinks or bald patches.

It would be fluffier the nearer you got to the base of his spine, and silkier and less fluffy toward the tip. The fluffiness near the base of his tail was continued into the region under his tail, thus giving rise to another of his nicknames: "Old Fluffy Bum". His body was slimmish, light and smoothly muscular, and somehow felt just like the body of a young child – a toddler – when you picked him up. He was a large cat – about a metre from nose to tail.

WHEN HE WAS A KITTEN he was pale ginger, softly fluffy, pretty thick, slow, lovable and very fond of being cuddled. Scarlett, who we got as a kitten at the same time as Pellinore (she was black and short-haired and from a different home) was much quicker and better co-ordinated than him and used to jump from chair to chair or up onto various surfaces with effortless accuracy and elasticity. Scarlett was actually so black she seemed the cat equivalent of a black hole; if the light was bad you had to locate her by sound. Her nature was very gentle, very sweet and exceedingly considerate and polite: she always sheathed her claws when close to you and never scratched, but she was also incredibly daring and adventurous – and a demon hunter, who always had to be locked up when fledglings were about. We would sometimes look out of the window at the bare alders at the end of the garden in winter and see a strange small, sinuous black shape weaving its way up near the trunk, or stalking along a branch 30 feet in the air: invariably Scarlett. Though she liked to be held in your arms and carried about, she never liked sitting on laps. She would very gently, carefully and apologetically remove herself from your lap and sit down on the sofa *beside* you, as if reluctant to hurt your feelings by an outright rejection.

As a kitten, when Ginge first saw Scarlett he thought she was wonderful and bounded straight up to her full of open, eager friendliness. But Scarlett came from an all-black litter, and maybe because of this she was terrified of Ginge and would fluff herself up, hiss horribly and hit him across the face with open claws. Ginge was always terribly surprised and rather hurt and would temporarily retreat, only to bound up again 10 minutes later, full of trust and friendliness: and receive exactly the same treatment. We seemed to be completely stuck in this impasse – it went on for days.

Then we decided to each take a kitten and play with it with a piece of string. Gradually we would draw the two bits of string and the playing kittens nearer and nearer to each other, hoping that because they were so bound up in their game Scarlett would forget her animosity, they would both start to chase the same string and that this common pursuit would teach them

they could get on together. It worked: Scarlett at first paused to hiss vigorously when she noticed Ginge nearby, but eventually she got too bound up in the game and in competing with Ginge to remember to dislike him. Suddenly they were running after the same piece of string, then there was touching of noses, lots of mutual washing, snuggling up and playfighting – and Ginge was flavour of the month.

Very soon Pellinore wanted to imitate Scarlett and jump in the lithe way she jumped, but due to his being so bumbling, uncoordinated and clumsy, this resulted in many humiliating falls, and general failures to get up onto things: a tendency to end up sliding down off the edges of sofas with ghastly scratching noises, or missing surfaces or the seats of chairs and crashing to the ground – a lot of general humiliation. Due to his bumbling nature, and also the quest he energetically set himself to emulate Scarlett, Malc decided we should call him

"Pellinore" after King Pellinore and the Questing Beast in T.H.White's *The Sword and The Stone*. I agreed it seemed to fit. So his Proper Name was Pellinore, though we usually called him Ginge or Gingeypuss (in addition to a large range of nicknames) as well.

But as Ginge grew into adolescence he kept copying Scarlett and following in her footsteps, and gradually became faster and more co-ordinated and lithe. Eventually he was as quick and good a jumper as she was. His jumping ability in the end was quite extraordinary. On holiday once in Cornwall, frustrated at being shut inside, from a standing start he jumped from the floor right onto the top lintel of an ordinary door, balanced on it a moment then jumped from it to a picture-rail-high shelf, about 5 feet away, that ran right round the room, and on which any number of fairly revolting ornaments were balanced. Then he began nonchalantly walking along the shelf, just *lightly grazing* the ornaments – producing exactly the panic-stricken reaction in Malc and I that he had hoped for, while effortlessly communicating his frustration and resentment.

Another time we were showing someone round the garden in summer and Ginge was just standing at our feet, having accompanied us down to the pond. A large blue Emperor dragonfly flew past us at about head height. From a standing start Ginge instantaneously leapt up into the air, clapping his paws together on a level with our heads: we were so astonished by such a leap that I do not remember whether he caught it or not. But it was not uncommon in summer to find a tangled iridescent mess on the lawn as a sign of this speedy and agile response.

Scarlett and Ginge were really just best mates. They went exploring and hunting together, ate together, cuddled up and slept together – and would no doubt have had kittens together if we hadn't intervened to have them spayed. Scarlett was initially the leader, though as time passed Ginge became increasingly independent and his own man. Had Scarlett lived as long as Ginge it's possible that he would not have become quite so psychologically and emotionally orientated toward us, but Scarlett died when she and Ginge were 3 years old and this had an enormous effect on Ginge when it happened.

IN THE GARDEN: FOXES AND KINGFISHERS

If Ginge was full of anticipation – a walk down the garden with us, a meal – he would walk quickly and deftly ahead of us his tail going straight up vertically into the air like a flag bearer. Sometimes he would arch the tip slightly over to the left as he walked. It made you feel you were following the hoisted tail down the garden path. This urge to lead was very marked and definite. Pellinore was not a follower, he was a leader of men and he knew it and he knew we knew it. We would obediently trot after him and wait patiently as all this confident and inspired leadership paused to elaborately sniff a bunch of grass, investigate an opening in the hedge or take a pee (with an air of great seriousness and concentration, always a discreet distance from us).

If we, getting a little impatient with our great leader's agenda, moved on, he would quickly hurry to catch up and overtake us in order to lead us back in the correct direction. If you picked him up on one of these walks, he was usually very pleased and amenable and would immediately use the elevated vantage point to scan the fields, garden or river, or anxiously peer ahead in the direction we were walking in case we hadn't smelt a particular scent or noticed some lurking vole in the undergrowth.

If something we couldn't hear or see drew his attention, he would begin to peremptorily wriggle and struggle, then jump down out of our arms, hurrying off to investigate. When he did that he usually had his claws out, very intent on getting some purchase on whatever texture was to hand – and if it was bare skin you would end up inadvertantly scratched. Despite many indignant displayings of blood to him over the years, this was an area where Pellinore remained uncharacteristically thick. He never managed to grasp the concept of sheathing his claws when jumping on or off laps, and we were both frequently covered in minor scratches and puncture wounds on our thighs, knees and upper arms as a result. Yet he was extremely good-natured and never lashed out at us with claws or teeth – any injuries incurred were purely incidental to us being landed on, or our trying to hang on to someone who was determined not to be hung on to.

Pellinore was a very macho, outdoors sort of cat. He loved to hunt, to explore, to go out all night, climb trees, walk on walls, watch the river, stalk along roofs, vault from branch to branch above a roaring torrent – in any weather. He would sit for hours by a hedge waiting for some godforsaken mouse or rat to make a move and in his time brought in most varieties of wildlife at least once, expecting gratitude and praise from us with resolute and unshakeable optimism. There was the once-off, enormous, totally intact mole that he dumped unceremoniously on the tiled floor in the kitchen while we were cooking supper. It had the most beautiful very fine, dense, silky black fur and retroussé nose and immediately went into what must be the default mole escape mode – it began going through the motions of *digging*, frantically. Since it couldn't get a grip on the tiles it simply spun round and round, while Pellinore sat watching it in deep fascination: he obviously didn't have a clue what to do with it now that he had caught it and expected us – as usual – to somehow *sort it out*.

We had long since dedicated an LP and a variety of plastic boxes to just such occasions, and quickly went off to fetch the largest box in the range. We shut the cats in and put the mole into the field nearby. The mole was lucky. Less lucky were the coffee-and-cream coloured stoats we found very occasionally (one in five years) lying in the garden. They were always uneaten and usually unmarked; it was more the way their corpses were casually dumped by a path or outside the back door that told us Pellinore was the culprit rather than natural causes. Since he could obviously kill stoats, it always seemed strange that he refused to tackle grey squirrels under any circumstances. Perhaps he had bitten off more than he could chew with a squirrel when he was young: at any rate, squirrels could openly taunt his authority and invade his territory, and he would simply sit and look at them with elaborate nonchalance, without making any response or advance. Although squirrels can be very fierce, I think stoats are much more so.

I once made Pellinore drop a teenage stoat he was about to bring into the house. It was about the size of a slim, half-grown rat. It lay curled on its side with its eyes shut as if dead. I went to get some leather gloves, intending to see if it was dead or alive and act accordingly. As I bent down towards it with outstretched hands it very suddenly jumped to its feet, drew its head back like a snake about to strike, and snarled and spat at me with incredible ferocity for something so small: I recall seeing a row of perfect miniature sharp white teeth. Then it shot off into a lavender hedge. I shut the cats inside and put a dish of cat food and some water down under the lavender. A few hours later the food was gone and there was no sign of the stoat.

On another occasion I was walking down the garden with Pellinore when we passed the gate into the field. He suddenly went all tense and crouched down in a very aggressive posture, then dashed through the gate down the steps into the field. Next second there was the most terrible squealing and caterwauling and Pellinore was locked in awful combat with something black and fluffy. For some reason I decided it must be a black kitten and set about trying to get Pellinore off it. I eventually succeeded in separating the two of them, only to realize as I did so that the "kitten" had a distinctive bullet-shaped head: it was a youngish mink, not a feline at all, and since mink are so destructive to all wildlife in and around the river, I thoroughly regretted my interference.

One of the most bizarre incidents involving Pellinore, Scarlett and other animals occurred one summer night a few hours after we arrived home from a journey to Scotland. We had done our usual route of Scotland to Gloucestershire on B-roads, minimising use of the M5 and M6 due to their absolute torpor-inducing terminal boredom and monotony. At some point on a small country road at about 2.00am, when it was night-time but relatively light, what appeared to be a large flock of birds suddenly flew across the road quite low, right in front of the car. The flock was so dense and the birds so large that we were afraid of hitting them and slowed right down. They were very black and began to flutter all round the car as they crossed our path. It was only then that we realized – with quite a shock – that the jagged outline of the birds' wings was all wrong – quite apart from the fact that flocks of birds don't usually fly about at night. It was an enormous colony of the biggest bats we had ever seen. They appeared very black and in my memory were about the size of crows – though how accurate this was, and whether their size was distorted by headlamps, shadows and the night, I do not know. It felt a very mysterious encounter: they came out of the night, briefly surrounded us, then disappeared again into the blackness. We felt we had somehow been fleetingly touched by some dark force of nature and were quite moved by the incident.

We drove on home, relishing the journey as usual, arriving back around 3.00am. That night we allowed Pellinore and Scarlett to come in our bedroom as they had not seen us for 10 days. Exhausted, we crashed out, oblivious to everything. While it was still completely dark I was suddenly woken by a strange bumping noise in the room. I lay in the dark, listening for a moment to these soft thumps that seemed to occur at fairly regular intervals – trying, in a befuddled way, to work out what was going on. Eventually I realized the cats were not on the bed and that what I was hearing was the sound of four paws taking off vertically, then flopping down onto the ground again. There was also a strange, very high-pitched squeaking. 4.00am??? With a groan I reached for the light, not knowing what I would find when I turned it on.

A *small bat* had flown in our open bedroom window and was now belting round and round the room at apparently supersonic speeds. Pellinore and Scarlett had positioned themselves on the carpet at two different points beneath the bat's flight-path, and as he zoomed over their wonderfully pert and wide-awake heads they took it in turns to leap up into the air, clapping their paws together in the air in their efforts to catch him. I had been woken by the sound of their sylph-like landings.

"Precious!" I shook Malc. "PRECIOUS!!!" "OOuummphh??!..." "There's a bat in the room!!!" "Whaaattt??!! ... O GOD ... I HATE bloody bats …". And he pulled the duvet over his head and sank back into unconsciousness. *Great.* There was no way I was going downstairs to get an LP and a plastic box at 4.00am after driving back from Edinburgh on B-roads. I got out of bed, opened the bedroom door, waited for the bat to fly into the hall, then smartly shut it again, vaguely hoping it would echo-locate out of some other open window. The strange coincidence of having been surrounded by a much larger species of bat earlier that night was not lost on me. Life was beginning to feel like a scene from *Love At First Bite.*

The next day, though we hunted everywhere, we could find no trace of the bat, and we decided that, once un-harassed by the cats, it had managed to find an open window and escape. But in the late afternoon I noticed Scarlett showing an uncharacteristic interest in the back of a portable gas fire on the hall landing – and when I investigated, sure enough, there was the little Pipistrelle Bat, suspended upside down from some metal-work near the gas-canister. I scooped it up in a tea-towel, carried it to the garden, then laid it on an LP which I held up as I stood on the lawn. On summer evenings there were often little bats flying about down by the river; this one must have followed some insect into our bedroom. It looked like a very ugly-sweet new-born kitten, but all brown and with a furry body, snub nose and tiny claws. Once it had got its bearings it skittered away through the air quite readily, none the worse for its experiences, and having provided us with a memorable coda to Bat Night.

In very cold frosty weather Pellinore often liked to stay out all night. We assumed that he had found a way into a neighbour's shed or something, but after several wintry-white early-morning hunts for him, it gradually dawned on us that he in fact spent such freezing nights curled up about 5 feet off the ground in a conifer hedge near the bottom of the garden. There was a place where, behind the encircling, dense foliage of the conifer boughs, three branches or trunks of the hedge had been sawn clean off, horizontally, all on a level with each other. Each sawn cross-section made a circular platform about 4″-5″ in diameter, with gaps of several inches between the three stems. Somehow Pellinore curled up in a ball on his side and balanced on top of these sawn-off trunks, in what seemed to us an incredibly uncomfortable position, and chose to spend sub-zero nights there. When we called him in the morning he would emerge either stretching rather sleepily from the bottom of the hedge, or give one of his very plangent, melodious meiows from his vantage point within it to call us over. Either way his body would be warm but his fur incredibly fluffed up, with a very cool, fresh, dry, ultra-buoyant sort of fluffiness. I think for him it was the equivalent of jumping in a freezing lake after the Finnish sauna of roasting his stomach against a radiator during the day. One of his nicknames was "Old Asbestos Paws" because of his penchant for lying on a coffee table for hours at a time, all four paws, with their dry, pale pink pads, pressed firmly against a radiator – which was too hot for us to touch for more than a second.

Pellinore, like many cats, was fascinated by water. He would sit in the bath trying to catch drips from the tap with his paws, or crouch on the edge of the bath and lean over to play with the water as it streamed out of the tap when one of us was taking a bath. He would do this until all the fur on his front legs was quite sodden and then he'd leave wet pawprints on the floor. If he came upon a hand-basin full of water he would crouch down, put one paw in the water and then paddle his paw as if doing front crawl, apparently trying to move the water from A to B, but in reality, I think, just enjoying the sensation of moving his paws through it. Once when the river flooded at the end of the garden and covered what was normally lawn for a space of 9 feet or so, Pellinore waded into the flood water just like a tiger, too interested to be concerned at getting wet, and began the "I move the water from A to B" paddling action that was normally reserved for the bathroom. Similarly he would wade into any gardening trays that were filled with rainwater.

Ginge was a keen gardener: if we were digging holes to plant bulbs or plants, he would closely observe: "share the experience" by looking with exaggerated interest into the hole, frequently supporting our work by leaning down and scraping the earth with his paws beside us, climbing into the hole, threatening to pee in it, or just raking earth about all over the place for the hell of it, with great gusto. He couldn't resist the bent back of hard labour: he would spring up onto our backs, then climb forward so he was draped, peering over our shoulders, purring encouragement into our ears as we worked. He would also start to play football with the bulbs, or grab anything we were using or planting and take off with it in his mouth like a dog hoping to be chased. He seemed to be a great believer in *group* endeavours and the power of a little calculated chaos to lighten things up, and was terrifically enthusiastic about watching *other people work*.

Although it was not unusual to glimpse foxes in the garden or adjacent fields from an upstairs window during the day, or to hear them on the lawn at night, on the whole I think Pellinore and Scarlett saw them off, so I have only had one close encounter apart from in a wildlife refuge. I was sitting in the garden reading one summer day accompanied by Scarlett, who was wandering around at my feet. Suddenly she assumed a rather threatened-looking posture and became very interested in the hedge about 2 yards from me. I got up to peer into the hedge in case she was after a bird, and to my surprise saw a large fox very calmly sitting inside the tangle of branches looking out at me – and the now spitting Scarlett. I wondered how long he had been there without Scarlett or I noticing.

Afraid they would fight, I clapped my hands and made a noise to frighten him away and he appeared to leave the hedge and run off through the far side into our neighbours' garden. I sat down to read again, assuming he had been frightened off, but a few minutes later I noticed Scarlett once more looking decidedly edgy, peering into the hedge. As I got up to investigate, Scarlett suddenly let out a dreadful caterwauling and leaped into the hedge. There ensued what can only be described as a ghastly cacophony of sound: a very shrill, high-pitched repeated barking, punctuated with yelping howls, completely mingled with the worst feline behaviour Scarlett was capable of, involving every kind of menacing growl, shriek and wail. I threw my book down and tore the length of the hedge to the gap where we could squeeze through to Greg and Mary's side of the garden if necessary. Then I ran back up on that side.

Scarlett and the fox (who was about three times Scarlett's size) were face to face: Scarlett crouching in an S-shape, the fox sitting on his haunches. Scarlett was swearing and snarling like a trooper and the fox, determined not to be outdone, was simply hysterically yapping into the air while glaring at her – like an overexcited terrier, but much louder. Though they were within inches of each other, neither of them was actually touching the other. As I ran toward them, I think I just *assumed* that my mere presence would break up the confrontation – but No.

I shortly found myself standing *right above* both Scarlett and the fox, who both totally ignored me and carried on with their shouting match as if I wasn't there. For a moment or so I didn't have the faintest idea what to do. "What will the neighbours think of all this noise?" was about as far as the pathetic brain activity went. The fox must have seen me, standing next to Scarlett right opposite him, and yet he totally ignored my presence. Scarlett was meanwhile getting more and more apoplectic with territorial indignation, but the more she shrieked and growled, the more the fox barked and squealed (or whatever it is fox noises are called.)

Eventually, through the ghastly racket, the Bridget Jones solution filtered into my head, and I shouted something like "Oi!!" and clapped my hands. There was this sudden silence – a real "Duh?" moment for the fox, as he looked up – and *finally* I got a bit of the Respect us homo sapiens assume is our God-given right. After a few more disgruntled yaps, the fox first backed away from Scarlett, then turned, and with a certain arrogant cool (though nowhere near as arrogant as a bloody mink) he ambled off toward the end of the garden, where he could get through the fence into the field. Scarlett was very fluffed up and insufferably pleased with herself, and I of course was very proud of her: but I banged her up immediately to avoid all possibility of injury and a massive vet bill.

During Scarlett's lifetime, when she and Ginge were young, catching birds was a problem with the two of them. However bedecked with collars and bells, they seemed to find a way, so we shut them in during the day when fledglings were about. By the time of Scarlett's death the birds in the garden had got to be very cat-wise, and the two of them were always marked whenever they went out. It seemed one or two birds would be deputised to continually monitor them and call out warnings that were noticed by all the other birds in the garden. Ginge could be found virtually anywhere by the scolding of one or two robins, wrens, blackbirds or tits. He rarely caught birds after Scarlett's death, even though the wagtails often swooped and danced over his head and moorhens wandered about the lawn each day. If he did, he usually laid them down gently, unmarked and very much alive, at our feet, whereupon he would be shut up and the bird returned to the garden. The sheer perpetual volume of robins, wrens, blackbirds, tits of all kinds, wagtails (they breed under the bridges), dippers, moorhens and jays in the garden, as well as rarer visitors, speaks of itself about how little overall effect the cats' predations had on the levels of wildlife. (Sparrowhawks took far more birds than Ginge and Scarlett ever did.) Ginge's real prey of choice was rats or mice and these he caught in abundance – to the extent that we often had a running scoreboard of "Us 3, Ginge 6", denoting how many mice we had been able to save from his clutches.

On the far side of the Trout Pool there is a kingfisher breeding site. The adults arrive to build their nest in early spring, before the leaves are on the trees, and at that time of year are easy to see as their vivid electric blue stands out very clearly against the greys and browns of winter. Usually we can stand on the bridge and watch them sitting around on branches outside their nest, or skimming away down-river if we cross the bridge too quickly because we didn't realize that they were there. On the

whole they are very shy, and we have to move slowly and not openly look at them when they are around if we want them to stay put.

Then, at leafburst, the kingfishers are harder to see. When they are stationary their colouring is so mobile and reflective that they are easily camouflaged by the varying greens of moving leaves, with their interplay of water and sunlit reflections. It's only when they fly in their characteristic very straight, linear flight-paths, that their brilliantly exotic (very un-British) colouring shows up. The vast majority of kingfishers tend to give piercing whistles as they fly, and one learns to identify the whistle and look up, so you can catch sight of them flying low over the garden or whistling along the entire loop of the river, passing under both our bridges with a flashy, supersonic grace.

Then one day, literally out of the blue, there won't be just two birds skimming the garden, or whistling to each other from opposite ends of the river's loop. Suddenly there are half a dozen, little, whistling, deeper brilliant-blue birds, flying up into the trees near the nest and fluttering about from tree to tree giving a juvenile version of the adult call. For about a day or two that we call The Flight of the Baby Kingfishers, the young kingfishers hang around in the trees and explore downriver, calling excitedly to each other and behaving – to my mind – in a totally un-kingfishery way: not at all shy. But kingfishers are, sadly, pretty useless parents, and after a cursory lesson or two in the art of fishing, they drive their young away to fend for themselves almost immediately. There is meant to be a very high rate of attrition in young kingfishers, though I have never found any dead young or adults.

GAMES

When they were kittens both Ginge and Scarlett liked to be put in a carrier bag or basket and then swung round and round through the air. They would jump into a bag and sit looking expectant until you picked it up and started to swing them to and fro – higher and higher – or else round and round, until you were too dizzy to go on. When you stopped they would both be purring thunderously. As a kitten Ginge would chase after thrown sticks and then bring them back to you, dog-fashion, for you to throw again. As he got older he appeared to think this game – especially the retrieving – a rather pointless exercise and refused to do it, sitting looking at you once he had reached (and disabled) the thrown stick, as if you were being pretty silly and immature to make all these "Come on Ginge, come on!!" noises.

Scrumpled-up pieces of silver foil, however, had an enduring fascination. When Malc especially crumpled up any piece of paper (but particularly foil), Pellinore would suddenly be rivetted with attention: all poised to spring after it in a split second. This was particularly funny when Malc had just been doing it quite unaware of Pellinore's presence – with a stock-cube wrapper while cooking, etc. If Malc threw it, Pellinore would fly off a kitchen surface, or launch himself with the utmost vigorousness across the floor, attacking the ball of paper with all the scatter-pawed, shotgun efficiency that he would bring to rat-catching, then biff and chase the paper the length of the hallway, bouncing it off skirting boards and doors with great accuracy and brio. In the end, the ball of paper inevitably disappeared under a closed door, oven or fridge. Pellinore would then either flop on his side with a "Well, that's that" sort of air, or sit bolt upright, staring alternately at the gap under the fridge/oven, then at whoever he expected to *retrieve* it for *him*. Another game he liked a lot was to flop down on his side either on the lino or on a wooden kitchen surface. I would then

bend down and spin him round and round at speed. After much spinning and purring this would turn into an orgy of tummy tickling where he would lie on his back with his paws in the air, exposing a vast expanse of pale, fluffy, warm ginger fur which it was very tempting to bury one's face in as it smelt of fresh laundry. I would also grab hold of his forepaws and wrestle with him and, if he turned over, lift up his back paws and turn him into a wheelbarrow. The front end of the wheelbarrow would then always make for the nearest food source.

His love of finding exotic places to sit or lie extended to many different scenarios and locations. Shelving systems of all kinds held an irresistible allure, and it sometimes seemed as if Pellinore deliberately sought out really funny places in which to sit, lie or curl up.

Once, when I was working at an animal refuge, I had bought a bird cage at the pet shop for keeping injured birds in. I brought it home and put it down in the kitchen, not noticing that one of the tiny 3"-5" square doors was open. No sooner was the cage deposited on the kitchen surface than Pellinore jumped up, took a good look at it, and immediately noticed this tiny door half-way up the side of the cage. Before I could stop him he had stuck his head through the door and raised one paw with which to follow it. I couldn't believe he could squeeze through the tiny gap, and as the first paw landed on the floor of the cage and the second front paw was raised I was seized with panic, thinking he would climb in and never be able to get out. (I had of course forgotten that the top and sides of the cage could be unclipped from the base tray if necessary.) Pellinore just climbed straight into the cage through its tiny aperture and sat down, purring. As usual on such occasions, we rushed for the camera.

Whenever we came in from shopping, Ginge would always want to welcome us home and be up on the surface helping us to unpack our purchases – often showing a pointed interest in absolutely any tins or cream-like cartons. If we left any empty carrier bags lying around, he would disappear head-first into them. Any cardboard boxes were likewise a magnet, to be climbed into from the top or side. Any flat box – whether it happened to be a pie or a pizza was totally immaterial – standing on top of another box or a fruit bowl, proved a siren call to Ginge, who took a pride in being able to climb on top of any pile, however precariously balanced, graciously sit down,

and survey the world purring, waiting for the shock-horror moment when we noticed. Sometimes these balancing feats were truly extraordinary, and no doubt a reflection of the idiotic absentmindedness with which Malc and I unpack after going to the supermarket. He would also lie down – in apparent blissful comfort – on things like a bag of potatoes or bulbs, or the tools from a toolbox, all pointed edges and very hard. He seemed to savour different textures to lie on, from the soft and fluffy to the downright excruciating.

Pellinore also loved to lick the empty wrappers of the organic stock cubes that we used, but being very light they had a tendency to travel frustratingly all over the kitchen when touched with his tongue. If we anchored the wrapper for him by picking up one of his front paws and placing it firmly on the edge of the wrapper, he would keep his paw there until it was licked clean, but he never seemed to remember to do this for himself in the first place.

After we had taken him on holiday just a few times, Ginge developed a really sharp capacity for "casing the joint". Once we were staying at a Yorkshire cottage on a farm with a lot of dogs about. Ginge was determined to get out and explore. We kept a window open in the very stuffy little bathroom: a small window at the top of a larger window that we kept closed. We never let the cats in the bathroom because of the open window.

One sunny day we decided to go and sit in the cottage garden about 10 yards from the house. We had inadvertently left the bathroom door ajar and before we had even sat down outside, Pellinore had streaked into the bathroom he had never been allowed in, jumped up over the lower window, climbed out of the open top window, and was there standing at our sides on the lawn. A while later it became apparent that there were dogs about, and having nosed around the somewhat ramshackle garden for a time, he raced back toward the cottage (one of a row), identified the precise high window he had climbed out of, leapt onto the window-sill, then up over the lower window and back in through the top one.

Pellinore was very nervous of any kind of male stranger, particularly workmen who made a noise. His favourite retreat in such stressful circumstances was the (first-floor) cupboard under the bathroom sink, which not only had an ample cupboard space but also gave on to a narrow gap between a wall and some cladding where he could hide even more safely. Having witnessed a couple of desperate, failed attempts on his part to scratch open the cupboard doors in order to escape a particularly demonic electrician, I decided to try and show him how to do it for himself. This involved standing him on his hind legs, placing one forepaw on each of the two knobs of the doors (side by side at the centre front), then getting him to give them both a quick *pull* at the same time to break the magnetic charge and open the doors. I ran through it a couple of times with him and sometime later he started a lifetime's habit of strolling into the bathroom, straight up to the cupbards, standing up on his hind legs, peremptorily pulling open both doors to either side of him and marching in. Many a visitor nearly choked on their toothpaste as Pellinore calmly plonked himself between their legs and went into this routine. He always did it with enormous aplomb and nonchalance – frequently not even bothering to enter the cupboards afterwards (just a quick inspection) but leaving all our toilet articles on open display. In time, because Sylvie often followed Ginge around, he also taught Sylvie how to perform this manoeuvre, and she does it to this day.

If *particularly* motivated he would occasionally break out of kitchens, or any other room he was shut in, by standing on his hind legs and turning door knobs with both paws, or pressing down horizontal handles to release the catches. If a door was shut and he (automatically knowing you were inside) wanted to come in, he would usually stand on his hind legs and rattle the door-handle by hitting it repeatedly with his forepaws and meiowing stridently. If you obediently opened the door, he would march unhurriedly past you into the room with a vague air of "Thank you, my good man, that will be all".

34

DUVETS, FRIDGES & TRACTORS

Pellinore was always *very* pleased if I was ill with a migraine during the day, because he loved to come and join me in bed. As the migraines could last for days at a time, with excruciating pain, nausea etc, he was a source of enormous comfort to me for many years. If I was not too floridly ill, but in a recovering state where he could keep me company, he really liked to burrow down under the duvet about on a level with my stomach. He would then lie there in the warm, purring loudly. After a while he would get too hot or short of air, and suddenly start to wriggle and push his way vigorously up through the folds of the duvet towards the top, emerge, turn and lie down on the bed.

But at some point he learnt that it was really rather nice to have a warm body and one's head coolly in the air (the windows were always wide open at such times, regardless of the seasons). So one day I woke up to find Pellinore asleep parallel to me, his body under the duvet and his head about 10″ from mine on the other pillow. The first time he just looked so funny I couldn't believe it, but it became a habit with him. We would lie like that together for long periods, often intermittently gazing into each other's eyes. All our cats are very keen on eye-contact, and Pellinore always seemed to have an innate understanding of the soul-value of sustained eye-contact. Indeed, when he was looking at you in this way with his pale aquamarine eyes, he would sometimes give small, inconsequential little mini-meiow noises, as if backing up the visual communication with a vocal element that had no purpose other than to add an indefinable something to the wordless exchange. After this, if Malc or I had left the bedroom door open, we would sometimes go in there during the day and find him lying in the bed, body under the duvet and head on the pillow, fast asleep.

Pellinore was particularly keen on any activity involving proximity to or opening of the fridge door, as the fridge was the Temple of Cream and Catfood. He would jump up on the surface above the fridge and time things so that, as you bent down to peer in at its contents for the butter or whatever, his head was always right there beside yours, and he was purring particularly seductively straight into your lowered ear. He also

would strike many different poses (shivering his tail with excitement), designed to signal exaggerated interest in absolutely anything you got out of the fridge – eggs, bread, Omega-3 oil. It didn't matter what we took out, since the object was a theatrical prop he used to *project* the keenness of his interest in the fridge's contents and generally remind us that this interest had not lapsed or died since the previous – all too distant – occasion an hour or a minute ago.

If we spent too long idly rummaging in the fridge, we would feel a firm paw placed between our shoulder-blades and the next minute Pellinore would be standing on our bent back, head still placed next to ours in that convivial, "let's share this exciting moment" posture, purring at top volume. The agony of trying to remove him oneself, while simultaneously trying not to stand up so that he dug his claws even harder into your back for *anchorage*, lingers vividly in the memory.

If at such times I decided to pour Ginge some goat cream, he would be so enthusiastic and eager to get at it that he would head-butt my hand as I was pouring it – possibly hoping for the surge and spill that inevitably resulted. If I said commandingly "WAIT!" he would back off; but it was a very hair-trigger thing, and at the slightest sign of weakening in me – a less stern expression, a lowered hand, turning away – he would race for the cream like a greyhound out of the starting gate. At such times he did what we called the "open-mouthed purr" which was a bit like a car without a silencer.

Indeed one summer I was sitting in the garden at the end facing the river on a very quiet day, and I heard the sound of a distant tractor. Since the muck-spreading and spraying doesn't confine itself to the fields, one automatically hunts around to check where exactly the tractor is and what it's doing. In this case the tractor appeared initially to be coming from one direction, and then abruptly to switch and be approaching from a different field. It was only when I got to my feet, puzzled, that I realized the tractor was in fact Ginge walking about behind me, purring very loudly.

Pellinore loved to hunt in the grassy field next to our garden and often we would look out of the kitchen window to see a tiny ginger dot – Ginge's head – sticking up out of a sea of green as he sat patiently waiting for some rodent to make a false move. In that same field a family of herons often came to rest, as it borders the river. They would sit upright and hunched, looking from a distance just like a group of large grey-and-white monkeys seated in the grass. Fortunately Ginge seemed naturally wary of these enormous birds: when they fly into the garden or over it, they often seem quite dragon-like in flight and descend in a soaring curve to land in an ungainly yet graceful lope of spindly legs, flapping wings and right-angled beak.

Often when Ginge raced the length of the garden back to the house he would, without slackening his pace, leap onto the wall by the Trout Pool and from there into the great Mountain Ash that has its roots in the river. There he'd vault, or chase

Scarlett, in an insane frenzy of exuberance, leaping from branch to branch, higher and higher up the tree, oblivious of potential hazards, while the water roared out of the mill race into the broad, deep pool below him.

But when there were cows in the field Ginge would become very nervous and scurry inside with his tail down, casting anxious backward glances in their direction. Scarlett, on the other hand, always fearless, would show off her devil-may-care nature by deliberately walking along low-hanging branches of the hawthorn or Perry Pear tree that bordered the field *right above the cows' backs,* looking down at them with casual curiosity and disdain.

SYLVIE

We had got Ginge and Scarlett as kittens within a week of each other – both at eight weeks of age. For Scarlett, the one week she had of being sole centre of attention made Ginge's arrival pretty miffing. After the initial challenge of getting Scarlett to accept Ginge through the medium of play, as I've described, they became great friends and did most things together, though occasionally Ginge would annoy Scarlett by being too boisterous and eager for horseplay. But they were really very devoted to each other and got up to all kinds of tricks.

Although we tried, when they were kittens, to make them afraid of the road beyond our house, and insist the road was off-limits, Scarlett was totally fearless of anything and to our dismay would occasionally emerge from bushes by the roadside 100 yards from our house and *run exuberantly down the middle of the road* in front of our car when we drove home, before racing into our front garden – as if it was all a great game.

Three years after we got her, Scarlett was hit by a car and though she managed to run into the house and upstairs to her favourite spot before lying down, she could not be saved. We were very sad. Before burying Scarlett we showed her body to Ginge so he would know what had happened. He came up to her, sniffed her body, then quietly moved a few feet away and crouched down with his back turned. All his usual high spirits and *joie de vivre* completely disappeared in the following 2-3 months. He sat about in the house or garden in a clear state of depression and sadness. Where he would usually race the length of the garden several times a day to come flying through the cat-flap like a bat out of hell, or wander along the river bank chasing leaves and hunting mice, or play frenetically in the house with his bits of scrumpled-up foil – now he just sat listlessly, doing no hunting whatever, and became very introverted and quiet, a real couch potato. We worried about him, but felt it was too soon to get another cat. He would purr when we talked to him, stroked or held him – but was much more passive than usual in his behaviour.

Eventually, after about 3 months, his spirits started to return and we thought of getting him another companion. Sylvie had grown up in a litter that lived in a summerhouse on a Cotswold hillside. Though we didn't realize it when we got her, she was very little socialised, and that mainly by unpredictable young children. As a result she would panic under certain circumstances, fluff herself up, hiss like a wildcat and strike out. We introduced Pellinore to Sylvie in the garden, so it was relatively neutral territory for Pellinore. He sat and looked at her stonily, without purring, his body language conveying he was distinctly underwhelmed. He spent a day or two ignoring Sylvie, washing, yawning, looking anywhere but at her – and

Sylvie, who was terrified of him, always hid under chairs or behind the sofa whenever she saw him. At length Pellinore must have decided she was not a threat, and while still keeping several feet away from her at all times he began to actively watch her – usually from the top of a table, chair, or kitchen surface, higher up than she was, looking down at her. Then he began to purr loudly as he observed her.

Soon Ginge was fairly fascinated by Sylvie, who was at this time very small but with large ears and paws that suggested she would grow to be a big cat like Ginge. We would distract

Sylvie with bits of string or whatever, so she didn't notice Ginge watching her and wouldn't run and hide – then, hopefully, he could become familiar with her presence.

Soon Ginge was willing to sit on the floor a few feet from the kitten, but Sylvie was still so frightened of him that she would always hide. We couldn't find a way to help her over her fear and were a bit nonplussed. But Ginge, who fearlessly fought rats, stoats and mink, and hadn't seen a kitten since he was one himself, showed remarkable tact. He would very deliberately go and sit down within view of where Sylvie was hiding, a few feet from her. Then he would put his tail straight out, pointing in her direction, but with his back to her, so he wasn't looking at her. He would then start, very gently, to twitch the end of his tail, up and down or from side to side, in a very mobile, strange way that he didn't normally do. Quite soon Sylvie would be rivetted by the twitching tip. Still too frightened to advance on it, she would peer out from behind table legs or from under sofas, obviously longing to investigate. Ginge never turned round or went towards her at this stage, he just sat hopefully twitching.

After a few goes Sylvie started to stalk Ginge's tail. As she emerged with great trepidation from behind her cover, and began to creep very low on the ground, behind his back, toward the twitching tail, Pellinore would inch it a little further away, keeping it moving most provocatively all the time – he seemed to know where she was without a direct line of sight. The nearer Sylvie, with enormous nervousness and hesitation, got to approaching his tail, the further Ginge would move it away from her in a 180-degree arc. If she crept all the way to one extreme, he would lift it up and swing it through the air so it landed, with elastic grace, back where it had been to begin with. He nearly always avoided looking at her directly, and behaved as if oblivious to her presence. It was a most extraordinary scene to witness and was repeated a number of times before Sylvie actually had the temerity to advance and make a move.

Eventually Sylvie was pouncing on Ginge's tail much as a kitten might its mother's. Ginge reacted with typical tact: a very spirited *use of tail* would ensue, with Sylvie flying after it, occasionally racing away to hide if something in Ginge's response pushed her beyond her comfort zone. Next Ginge began to wash Sylvie's ears and generally show an intensely maternal side, and she started to love cuddling up next to him. Afterwards, throughout their life together, Sylvie often went up to Ginge and shoved her head under his nose demanding to be washed. However she was totally disinterested in ever returning the favour, and her rather demanding behaviour sometimes irritated Ginge in later years, and he would then either be rather grumpy and grudging about washing her ears, or else simply duff her over instead.

Given that Ginge was so keen on relating to people and so dog-like in his behaviour and outlook, it always seemed strange that it was Sylvie, not Ginge, who eventually developed the well-known animal capacity for knowing when her "owner" was coming home. I had to commute 12 miles by car to work, and the time I came home varied considerably, due both to variable hours and traffic conditions on the return drive. Yet as I drew up in our driveway, I could almost always see Sylvie's grey shape sitting the other side of the see-through glass door into the kitchen where we entered the house, waiting.

Malc was once fetching something from an adjacent room when Sylvie walked very purposefully past him into the kitchen. Knowing (as he thought) I wouldn't be home for a couple of hours that day, he followed her to see what she did. She took up her position at the door and waited. Malc then realized I had probably left earlier than I had planned, and decided to wait and see if I appeared. About five minutes later I drew up in the car, having been poleaxed by a migraine and needing to get home early before it got too bad for me to drive.

On such occasions Ginge might – or might not – sleepily emerge once the door banged, or thunder downstairs because he thought some tea might be in the offing when he heard voices – but it was Sylvie who always kept watch, and waited, and still does so.

HIS MEIOWS

When he was young Pellinore had a very loud, pure, bell-like meiow, very plangent, soulful and melodious – extremely musical. If he felt insecure or neglected, he would stand at the bottom of the stairs and release a series of these very carrying, soulful meiows, pausing a little between sonic balloon-launches to gauge the effect of his call on us. It was unmistakeably a contact-call, and he would confidently expect me – upstairs in my study – either to call out loudly "PELLINORE!!", or better still, to *meiow back*. (Malc's study was out of earshot.) There would then follow an exchange of human/feline calls going back and forth. If he just wanted to establish contact, he would at this point race up the stairs with an exhilarating thunder of paws, burst into whatever room you were responding from and take a flying leap onto your table or lap, scattering any work in progress without hesitation.

If the contact call had a downstairs motive – such as a closed cat-flap, or an overwhelming desire for food – he wouldn't move from the spot, but would make the meiows progressively more soft, plaintive, widely spaced and *disappointed*, the longer you refused to comply with his wholly reasonable request. He had his paw on the pulse to such an expert degree that this point of blatant refusal to respond was rarely reached. But if you did refuse, when you finally went downstairs he had usually gone out and would either reappear sometime later with an aggravating mouse, or be very interested in washing and simply ignore you for a while. But he could never keep this up for long, because he was too good-natured and friendly. After a couple of strokes or being picked up, he would break out in a loud purr in spite of himself.

Sylvie never seems able to deliver a really loud, full-bodied meiow (except when she is about to be sick). She always makes

a sound we call "quacking", because it consists of screwing her face up, opening her mouth wide, then giving an "--eh!" sound. If we then go "--eh!!" to Sylvie, she goes "--eh!!" back and the exchange can go on indefinitely. It can even become a very trying monologue *all through the night* if she is sleeping on your bed. About 6 years after Sylvie started doing this, Ginge observed that we spent a lot of time "quacking" at Sylvie and exclaiming how sweet her quack was, so he appeared to decide to change his meiow to something that would earn him more attention. He then started to give a very silly, extremely high-pitched *squeak*, virtually like a mouse. This must have earned him a lot of interest, because the squeak became an alternative meiow for him – in addition to a very large range of other meiows and vocalisations. If he was shut in the other side of the house and you opened the door to call him, you would often hear a series of fantastically silly squeaks punctuating a loud drumming of paws as he came racing exuberantly down the stairs.

Pellinore's particular meiow to tell us he had caught a rat or mouse was like a somewhat (necessarily) muffled and sinister version of his melodious meiow. But it ended on a *downward* note instead of on a note of enquiry: it was a simple statement of fact. One learnt to leap out of the chair pretty sharpish when you heard this meiow of **announcement**, because otherwise he would chase the rat/mouse round the kitchen or the house. It might end up dying in some extremely inconvenient refuge, where its rotting corpse would have to be located and removed from behind a 10 by 6 ft bookcase, or a section of the back of the kitchen cupboards cut away to get it out.

Before he went out of the cat-flap during the early evening, he had a characteristic short, rather creaky-sounding meiow that was a "Bye for now, see you!" signature which he'd give to whichever of us happened to be there cooking supper or clearing up. We'd give the equivalent meiow back. Sometimes this had a particularly perfunctory quality, as if he could hardly be bothered to say it, and we learnt to recognise that this meant he'd only be gone for a minute as he was just taking a *quick pee*. If he came in, not terribly enthused with the evening's work or hunt, and was in a rather subdued "Where have all the bloody mice gone?" mood, he'd climb through the cat-flap relatively slowly, one paw at a time, tail down, and give one quick, short, quiet, rather plaintive cry, before jumping up on his kitchen surface and washing without purring or seeking contact.

When he happened to be up on his surface, at times when we had come into the kitchen but had been too preoccupied to notice him or think about important things like *snackettes*, he would seek to get our attention by making a hoarse-sounding, staccato, quickly repeated relation of a meiow that came from the back of his throat. It was not unlike some water-bird's call. It had no resonance. If you turned and responded to it, Pellinore, having given this call from a sitting position, would rise to his feet, brushing his head firmly against your hand, rearing up as you stroked him (as was his habit) and purring abundantly as if to reward you for turning around.

Another form of meiow was one which usually accompanied a particularly dramatic entrance – where, say, we had been out all day and just come in and he had raced downstairs to greet us, or when *he* had been outside and had a nice time, and wanted to communicate the good news to *us* as he came in. For this he would begin meiowing some 30 feet away outside (or further, if he was in the house), long before he even hit the cat-flap or came through the door of the room. It would start off very melodious and very loud, but not plangent or lingering, and would be repeated at intervals of ever-decreasing length. So the meiows came faster and shorter the nearer he got to you, until he would leap onto the arm of a chair, or some surface, timing the last meiow to end on a breathless note as he looked you full in the eye, shivering his tail with excitement and happiness and purring at top volume, often butting you with his head. (The coming-down-stairs-with-a-series-of-idiotic-squeaks meiow was a late variant on this.) Happiness and enthusiasm were almost invariably a hallmark of everything he did; and, not being similarly gifted, we valued Pellinore all the more highly for this most precious quality.

Quite often I was so afraid something might happen to him in the night, and we would never see him again, that I would shut the cat flap before going to bed so he couldn't go out. As soon as he saw me do this, he would jump off his kitchen surface, go to the cat flap, sit down in front of it, and meaningfully and with great dignity STARE unflinchingly at it. Or else he would stand and raise a front paw and thump it against the closed flap while looking up at us – as if pointing out to us what we already knew: that it would not open. This latter performance would be accompanied by many accusatory, loud, plaintive but defiant mieows and indignant glares, with an air of "Surely there must be some mistake here? – I have urgent business outside". It was a battle of wills – and Pellinore usually made us feel so awful for banging him up so unreasonably that he won.

Ginge's vocal range and inventiveness was very varied and often surprising. It was as if he knew that every sound he made was potentially a form of communication and he continually experimented to find out what worked. Another of the noises he made couldn't really be categorised as a meiow at all – as it was an *absence* of a meiow. He usually used it when he already had your attention, but needed to convey a further point that you hadn't yet picked up. This could be a demand for CREAM *as well as* catfood, or wanting to get you to *not only* open a door, but come in the garden with him too. It didn't really matter what, it was a "NOT ONLY – BUT ALSO" meiow. This he gave by looking you squarely in the eye, standing up and leaning toward you, raising his tail, then opening his mouth and miming the shape of a meiow – without letting any sound come out. Then, when you looked at him enquiringly, he would lean forward again, looking beseeching, and repeat it. If he didn't follow it up with a movement in any direction, but just stood there doing this and reached toward you with a front paw, it could also be the cue for him wanting a particularly focussed sort of love-in, where he was asking you to pick him up and have a good cuddle instead of cooking the stupid bloody dinner.

Before I deal with the "Look out – I've taken LSD!" and "I am about to vomit semi-digested rat" meiows, there is another distinctive mode of musical communication I should mention. This was what we called "The Protest Meiow", and was delivered with a very widely-drawn mouth, showing the incisors; if he was standing, his tail would be held fairly horizontal with a bit of a droop, ears tending to twitch back, eyes blazing straight at you in a fixed and determined stare. The classic situation for it was when he was "grounded": if for some reason we didn't want him going out when he *very* much wanted to, or if we weren't allowing him to do something he was *very* set on doing and he knew we were forbidding him to do it. It was the feline equivalent of dragging your nails down a blackboard, and it played on the nerves in a very similar way, modulating between a couple of notes that might have been a sharp and a flat – the kind kids use when they grizzle, but higher. Fortunately he didn't feel the need of this communication tool terribly often – mainly it was when there were birds to protect or truly terrible storms and the river was in full spate, and only a total maniac would want to go outside.

The last two meiows I remember were the "I've taken LSD" and "I am about to vomit regurgitated rat" meiows. The former was mercifully rare, a kind of loud, fitful WAILING usually accompanied by very exhibitionistic, insane behaviour of a rock-star-smashes-up-hotel variety. The latter was a ghastly, plaintive, and no doubt regretful HOWL that was the signal for everyone to rush for a newspaper, or at any rate get Ginge OFF THE CARPET.

PLAYING WITH OTTERS

Although we have had frequent signs over the years of the presence of otters in the garden, we have only actually seen them twice, both times at very close quarters. Usually it is mainly otter tracks in the snow (with their distinctive tail-drag and claws), or a trail in the dew, cutting across the lawn in winter to stop abruptly on the river bank. The tracks go from the steps by the Trout Pool (where the mill-race pours out a torrent of very fast water), through a hedge and across our garden to a point further up-river beyond the mill-race. The mill-race is a 20-foot-long, narrow, high-walled, tilted gulley about 6 feet wide and 6ft deep, with a tremendously strong current when it is swollen and in full spate. The otters appear unable to get up-river if the current in the mill-race is too strong, so they cut across the garden to bypass it.

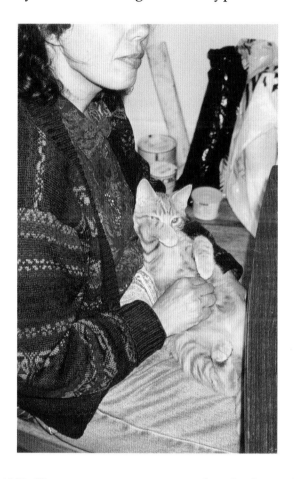

Normally if Pellinore came across any kind of interloper in the garden his body language would become very tense and aggressive. Ears flattened, he'd freeze or put his body very low to the ground, a stalking posture: then he'd give a very low but audible growl and plain *charge*, at which point his fur would fluff up and all hell would break loose. He was extremely territorial and highly aggressive in defence of what he regarded as his – or our – territory.

One early winter morning I had gone out to put some bird seed on the sundial near the centre of our garden – across the bridge over the mill-race, beyond a stretch of lawn. I was sprinkling the seed onto the sundial when something made me turn round and look back in the direction of the house.

As I did so I saw a strange, brown creature about the size of a half-grown Labrador (but on shorter legs), with magnificent whiskers, emerge from the bushes near the Trout Pool steps and walk across the grass parallel with the mill-race. I was so surprised, I couldn't think what it was, and as I stared various attempts at identification flitted quickly through my head. Stoat? no; mink? – too brown and big, head wrong; rat? – far too big, etc. Then I realized I was looking at a medium-sized adult otter, soaking wet from the river, who was walking in a totally unhurried, rather plodding way across the garden not 12 feet from me.

At the very moment I realized this, I also saw Pellinore step off the bridge at a point that gave him a direct view of the otter. I saw his body become alert as he caught sight of the interloper. Knowing both that otters are extremely strong and can be very fierce, and that Pellinore was highly territorial, I was immediately afraid they would fight. Even as I watched, Pellinore ran toward the otter – but not aggressively. He ran forward as he would if he were trying to get Scarlett to play with him, and when he came level with the otter he didn't hiss, or fluff up, or adopt any kind of aggressive posture, he just sort of gambolled along at the otter's side – as if inviting the otter to play. The otter turned his head briefly toward Pellinore, then carried on walking, totally unconcerned.

All this quality of interaction I only registered in hindsight: at the time I was so convinced there was going to be *slaughter* that I was hurrying to catch up with them in some vague hope of averting disaster. Pellinore and the otter disappeared some 5 feet ahead of me through a gap in the hedge which divided our garden from our neighbours'. As I passed through the gap I saw them move across another 20 feet or so of grass: Pellinore gambolling playfully at the otter's side – while the otter pretty much ignored him, as if to say "Not today, Pellinore, I have more pressing matters to attend to this morning". Having reached the far bank, the otter dived seamlessly off it into the river and disappeared from view – leaving Pellinore standing looking hopefully out over the water with his ears pricked forward and his tail in the air.

The second otter sighting was actually in summer, the year (2007) that we had bad summer floods. Because of the heavy rain the mill race was uncharacteristically full and fast for summer, and on that particular day it was a lovely morning. Malc and I were sitting out on an area where we often breakfasted when the weather was fine. (It was a few feet from the sundial where I had stood the first time I had seen an otter.) It looked toward the mill race and the bank where the first otter had returned to the water. (In the intervening years we had bought our neighbours' side of the house and removed the dividing hedge). We were really just finishing breakfast: Pellinore had exuberantly leaped onto Malc's lap while he was peeling an apple, and Malc was trying to prevent the apple getting ginger fur all over it and negotiate past the tail-plume waving in his face to continue peeling.

Once again, something made me turn my attention from Malc and Pellinore and look over my shoulder to my right. This time I had no problem recognising what I was seeing. The most *enormous* otter was walking across the grass about 6 feet away from me. He was absolutely in his prime, and his coat, perfect and sleek, gleaming with water, glistened at every step he took in the morning sun. I was just amazed – at the otter's presence, his closeness to us, his size, his beauty – but the next second I remembered Pellinore. I quickly glanced back at Malc and Pellinore and realised that Pellinore had seen the otter and was going to jump off Malc's lap. I believe I cried out as Pellinore – as was his habit – sank all 20 claws in Malc's thighs in order to get *really good lift-off* as he leapt into the air after the creature.

As Pellinore jumped, I hurriedly got up, swerved round the patio table and, once again, ran after Pellinore and the otter. As with the previous encounter I had witnessed, neither animal showed any sign whatever of aggressive, or even defensive, behaviour. This otter moved slightly faster than the first one, I was aware of the curving motion of its back, but it had no overt sense of being in a hurry, fully aware of the ginger cat 8"-10" from him, but unconcerned; while Pellinore gambolled beside and a little in front of him, constantly trying to engage the otter in play. Eventually they reached the river bank and the otter melted into a hedge that bordered it at that spot, and they both disappeared. When I caught up, Pellinore was still standing inside the loose-knit branches of the lilac hedge, looking wistfully at the unperturbed water.

Unfortunately when Pellinore jumped off Malc's lap, he did it with such unbridled enthusiasm that Malc, who hadn't seen the otter, shut his eyes and yelped with pain. When he finally opened them, all he could think of was his wounded thighs and he was totally bemused as to why I had suddenly rushed away from the table in hot pursuit of Pellinore – and was bitterly disappointed when he learnt why.

The impression I took away from these two encounters was that the otters knew Ginge well. From the way Pellinore behaved from the moment he caught sight of either otter, I'd guess that one reason he was so keen to go out at night was because he loved to play with the otters – and otters certainly like to play: not only with each other. In 2009 there was a picture in *BBC Wildlife Magazine* of a fox and an otter playing during daylight hours. I think it very likely that with otters passing regularly through the garden at night or at dawn (they are on our river to either side of us), Pellinore at some point became fascinated by them and then befriended them – or vice versa. In hindsight I think the first otter was a female and probably older than the second one – who I believed to be male and in his prime.

Pellinore was also fascinated by frogs, tadpoles and toads. He never killed or ate any that we knew of. In 14 years he only ever brought one frog into the house – a very large, beautifully patterned Common Frog that hopped about on the kitchen tiles in erratic 10" leaps. Pellinore meanwhile sat watching, quite upright, with his head going from side to side in unison with the frog's movements – until we caught it, shut Ginge up, and put the frog into the field margin by the river.

But one spring we went for a walk in bluebell woods near Marlborough with some friends. The weather had been very

wet a few weeks before, but we had since had quite a run of beautiful sunny days. The bluebells were an undulating blue mist right through the entire woodland. We came to a path which had deep ruts where a vehicle had cut through mud. The ruts had evidently been filled with rain and some enterprising frog had laid *tons* of frogspawn in them. Unfortunately the good weather had all but dried out the ruts and now they were filled with hundreds of wriggling and dying jet-black tadpoles, desperately trying to compete for the remaining small pools of muddy water. We were a long way from the car, but someone produced a water bottle and we scooped up as many tadpoles as we could to take back home to our pond.

So that the tadpoles wouldn't immediately be eaten by the many totally *Jurassic* Emperor Dragonfly nymphs in the pond, we put them in filtered pond-water in a washing-up bowl in the upstairs bathroom, where we fed them on boiled lettuce. It quickly became Pellinore's main objective in life to break into the bathroom and find out *what we had taken in there that he wasn't allowed to see.* In the end we got so sick of the battles to block his access when we took the tadpoles their lettuce, that we scooped Pellinore up and carried him, purring thunderously (he was always quick to recognise when he'd scored a victory), into the bathroom. We put him down next to the bowl and he was immediately and predictably *rivetted* by the wriggling tadpoles. A ginger paw whipped out and hovered over the water, ready to strike. "No, Pellinore, NICE TADPOLES, OUR tadpoles, NOT Pellinore's tadpoles." He'd glance up at us, lower the paw to the table and continue looking. A few seconds later he'd start surreptitiously to move his front paw again, as if unaware that it was attached to him, but simply had a life all of its own.

As soon as it was in the air we would take hold of his paw and put it down on the table again, saying "NO. NICE tadpoles, DADDY'S tadpoles, NOT for Pellinore". This whole performance was repeated two or three more times with varying words or actions, but Pellinore knew damn well, if only from our tone, that the message was clear: DON'T MESS WITH THE TADPOLES OR YOU'RE OUT.

He took to assiduously accompanying us, dog-like, on our trips to feed the 'poles ("TADPOLES, Pellinore? TADPOLES??!!"), leaping up effortlessly onto the small table to sit by the washing-up bowl and peer down at the frisky inhabitants. After the first day or so he seemed to take a pride in virtuously never putting his paws into the water or even raising them, but would sit there purring, placidly gazing down at them, a

picture of appreciative benevolence – though we didn't take any chances, and never left him alone with them in case he was suddenly overwhelmed by temptation. Later, when they finally emerged from the pond and were hopping about the garden as little froglets, he would closely follow and observe them, but didn't touch them.

HOW INTELLIGENT IS YOUR PET???

One year there was a sort of Pet Intelligence survey on one of the nature-orientated programmes on TV. It set out a range of simple tasks or tests that people could do with their pets, designed to explore their pets' aptitude in those matters. There were probably snack-rewards, etc. built into the whole game.

As Pellinore had shown himself so ingenious, adept, and generally ace over the years in so many ways, Malc and I were pretty taken with the idea of doing the tasks and demonstrating his prowess, even though we believed that such tests are often worthless and tell us more about humans than they do about the animals.

Unfortunately, in the true spirit of scientific enquiry, I can't recall the precise format of the TV tests, but I think some consisted of putting bits of kibble under things and then hiding things and so on – all very simple stuff. What I *do* remember, is

Pellinore sitting bolt upright and staring at each of the test scenarios we presented to him (in ever-increasing, pleading frustration) with a kind of stupefied blankness and an air of utter non-engagement. Far from scoring 10 out of 10 or even 3, 4 or a ghastly 1, he achieved a resounding 0000000 on every test, on all fronts, and demonstrated a sort of mega-genius-level obtuseness in relation to the tasks: which were of a kind he would normally do without thinking on a daily basis. Usually the promise of food alone would guarantee a certain degree of alert responsiveness and ingenuity on his part, but at the end of the day we were left with no option in relation to this memorable TV programme but to assume that Pellinore was, *quite undoubtedly, <u>and officially</u>,* incredibly thick.

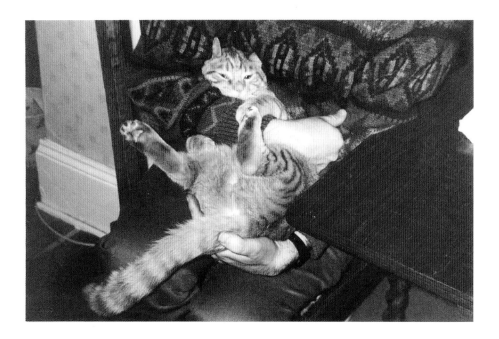

There were other occasions when Pellinore demonstrated a certain bloody-mindedness. In general Ginge was very sociable when he knew people, and would often come into the sitting-room and introduce himself, and be affable and charming, gracing laps etc; but there usually came a point when he felt the guests had had enough attention and it was time they were gently moved along.

He'd deliver the "I'm not getting enough attention, so it's time for you to go" message in a variety of subtle or not-so-subtle ways. There was the time-honoured feline strategy of jumping very publicly onto high and deeply forbidden places where precious cat-vulnerable ornaments are housed, and casually sauntering among them with an air of absent-minded, careless curiosity. Or leaping into the centre of a very cluttered dining table in mid-meal with six people round it, and seamlessly flopping down on his side so salt, pepper, sauce, cream, glasses etc were all knocked for six; then stretching out and purring seraphically, surrounded by shrieking diners. Or suddenly racing round and round the room at a minimum of 120m.p.h., leaping from the arms of chairs to backs of sofas, springing off shoulders, laps, even occasionally *heads*, in order to gain momentum – in short doing anything he could to create absolute pandemonium until he was abruptly turfed out of the room, having made his point. Then he would stalk off into the garden, locate some unfortunate not-a-good-Christmas mouse, and when he saw the door to the dining room full of guests was once more ajar, creep in with the mouse and set it free.

All these strategies for nudging guests on their way had been seamlessly perfected over the years – it was a well-worn routine. But one year he felt the unique disruption caused by Christmas preparations demanded something special, something really *memorable*. Malc and I were doing the presents and had laid them out in a long row ready to be wrapped and transported to London. Ginge was mollocking about in a disgruntled way – attacking the balls on the Christmas tree, pulling silver shred off it with his claws, charging into sheets of wrapping paper where they lay on the carpet, pulling off mouthfuls of glittering scraps and tossing them into the air, then running like hell whenever we said "**GINGEY-PUSS**!!!! NOW THAT'S **ENOUGH**!!! **STOPPITTT**!!!" – He was really pushing his luck, and he knew it.

He actually loved to help us with the Christmas cards by lying on top of them or on our address books, gently patting the odd packet of cards toward the edge of the table and watching with innocent astonishment as it fell on the floor. If we tried to lever out a card from under him it would become a game of tug-of-war, the card eventually bearing the hallmarks of velociraptor attack. If we were writing inside the cards, this was a cue to lend power to our elbows by clutching the pen with his paws and chewing the end of the biro with sharp, cracking noises that made you fear for his teeth. He would also lie on top of the cards with his paws in the air, looking at you upside down, wriggling playfully and reaching out to you with his paws. If that didn't work, as a last resort there was the sudden "I must just wash my back" four-pawed pivot from one position to another, which necessitated sweeping every card in a radius of 10" off the table with an *urgently graceful* coiling motion.

On this particular occasion, having gone through most of his Christmas repertoire, Pellinore was suffering badly (though not as badly as us) from Bored Cat Syndrome. He had probably been thrown out of the room at least twice. He came back in, superficially chastened, had a quick wash, then sauntered quietly over to our satisfying row of Christmas presents that awaited wrapping.

Knowing he was in a bolshy "Whether I come with you or stay here, I *hate* the disruption of Christmas" mood, we kept an eye on him. He wandered down the line, casually sniffing the odd item as if inspecting it, glancing up at us where we sat at the table writing cards as he lowered his head to sniff. He arrived at my most prized present of the year, a lovely blue shirt for my nephew Alex.

I said, in a warning tone, just in case he decided to rake it with his claws in a fit of endearing exuberance, "PELLINORE ..." whereat in one seamless movement he moved onto the shirt, squatted down, raised a quivering tail, gave me a fleeting, defiant glance, then fixed his eyes heavenward in clouded concentration. By the time I had shot across the room, swearing horribly, the terrible deed was done, and Alex's beautiful present was completely soaked in cat pee – something Pellinore had never done in the house before (or since) outside a litter tray – and Ginge had fled at top speed out of the room, into the kitchen and straight out the cat-flap with a loud BANG.

"WASHING!!??!!"

Pellinore was a very clean cat, who could lick off any amount of mud, dirt, and ghastly indeterminate substances, and while liberally depositing them on the carpets, be wonderfully spotless in himself. This enthusiasm for personal hygene also included an intense interest in *our* washing habits. Having found on many occasions that as soon as I was remotely naked in the bathroom, Pellinore was perched at my side, I took to saying to him around breakfast-time "Washing??!!Washing??!!" He would look at me alertly and then (if he was in the mood) belt upstairs, and sit waiting for me on the tiles beside the handbasin.

He would sit upright watching the taps being turned on, the bath or basin filled with water, the soap moistened, all with enormous concentration. He displayed an intense interest in ablutions (his head moving up and down as he followed the soap's movements), that generally only waned with the drying stage – when he would finally flop down on his side on the tiles, usually getting his fur or tail in the wet soap, and then lie there purring in a somewhat louche, steam-soaked manner while I got dressed. Apart from the occasional paw-dabbling in my washing water, or walking precariously along the edge of the bath to drape himself over a wet corner, there did not seem to be any reason for this enthusiasm other than an extension of his love of togetherness and convivial sharing of activities – and his fascination for water.

If we put down clean drinking water for him – always, preferably, in a metal bowl – he would first stir the water around thoroughly with his paws before drinking it: to such an extent that we had to have a plastic tray under the bowl to prevent the floor getting watermarked by the perpetual lake surrounding it. The bottom of the bowl often bore small traces of grit and debris from his paws.

When you picked Ginge up he would mould himself to the shape of your body, always turning his face to the left. He would tuck his head under my chin, close to my neck, and purr and purr, holding onto my upper arms with his paws. In this position he could be raised up or lowered very easily if I wanted to kiss the top of his head or bury my face in his fur. He always gave off a sense of rapturous enjoyment and pleasure and love of this closeness, which in turn made whoever held him feel really happy. It was a wonderful bond that he could create instantaneously, and call up from nowhere in a second. If you were sitting down he would jump on your lap without any hesitation – an inalienable right, an automatic assumption of being wanted. He would either flop right down in whatever position suited him or, at other times, turn round and round on the spot, carefully selecting the most comfortable angle of approach and articulation of leg and lap.

On these occasions he particularly liked to be picked up, turned to the left, and nestled in the crook of one's arm, so all four paws were pointing off to the left together. You could stroke his tummy or hold 'a whole bunch of paws' in one hand.

He would regress into a baby-like, kittenish state, purring dreamily, utterly relaxed, often starting to snore after a while. If he suspected that, although he wanted to settle on your lap, you had another agenda (like actually having to get washed and dressed in the morning for work), he would do what Malc and I called his 'instantly asleep act' – jump on lap, curl up in ball, close eyes, snore – all in the space of about ten seconds. He knew that a cat that is fast asleep is more likely to preserve its lap than one that is awake and thus fit to be turfed off.

If Ginge wanted to be picked up and cuddled or made much of and you were oblivious to the warning cues (particularly when he was young), he would simply launch himself through the air – like a prop thrown by a prop-man from off-stage left – and land on whatever bit of you was to hand, whether vertical, horizontal, half on or half off. This included those occasions when you were carrying hot drinks, plates of food, laden trays, milk bottles, books, boiling casseroles etc etc, and it was often a matter of dodging the flying cat before he added unique interest to the evening meal or splattered the sitting room wall with molten coffee. When in this state of heightened need both he and Sylvie would be totally blinkered about *context*. I was once sitting on a bar stool trying to open a large pizza box to get the pizza out when first Ginge flew over my shoulder and landed on top of the (thankfully still closed) box, closely followed by Sylvie's (then) enormous bulk. They proceeded to vie with each other to curl up and *lie down* on top of the pizza(until rudely removed by Malc), and since they were both extremely large – and in Sylvie's case very heavy cats – the

73

pizza was eventually much the worse for wear, with its 'Hawaian' ingredients all squished up one end.

As is the case with most cat owners, I am sure, we realized that a lot of what we picked up of Ginge's moods was revealed by his ears, tail and whiskers. The ears in particular seemed to fulfil the function which, in humans, is performed by the eyebrows. They performed a virtual semaphore indicative of mood. A lift of an eyebrow in a human translates into the backward twitch of one ear in a cat. The level of descent of human brows – the further down, the blacker the mood – translates, in a cat, into the irritation of two backward flattened ears, and so on. When this was accompanied by a twitching or lashing tail, we knew Ginge was seriously miffed. Likewise the positioning of Ginge's whiskers could be read like the position of a person's mouth. Just as a grin can be wry or heartfelt, so a pair of whiskers lying flattish against the cheeks could denote mild impatience or warm contentment, depending on context. If the whiskers were relaxed and standing proud, usually he was too. Pellinore's whiskers, ears and tail all felt as if they were very eloquent, very sensitive and informative in the arena of communication.

Ginge became fairly obsessed with our pond when we first made it, and went round with semi-permanently wet front paws, but after a while the glamour faded and he simply took to lying on top of the plank we had placed across the pond to enable us to reach down into it to position pond-plants, etc. There he would bask in the sun, evidently very satisfied and happy to be lying *above* water, just as he loved to lie on the small jetty that jutted out over the river at the end of the garden.

At some point we thought we might try and make the pond look really superior and do some kind of Rosemary Verey-style old stone edging to it. In order to get a sense of how it might look we dumped an old flagstone that had been lying around the garden down beside the pond. The result looked just like – an old flagstone dumped by a pond, and evoked absolutely none of the full-blown English Romantic charm we had envisaged. However Sylvie, who had long had a passion during summer for rolling on her back on the concrete patio outside the kitchen, thought it was absolutely wonderful. Sylvie was, at this point in time, appallingly overweight. Her weight just mushroomed after she was spayed, and Ginge's habit of bringing in mice at all hours for her to eat didn't help with our attempts to put her on a diet.

So Sylvie was virtually *round* in those days (though she is definitely not like that now), and looked incredibly funny when she rolled about – four legs sticking up, flailing around in the air, out of this striped *furry vastness*, but all done with terrific abandonment and gusto. Anyway she took to rolling on this flagstone we had laid down by the pond to Verey-fy it. Once she got going, there was no stopping her – it must have been something in the texture of the stone in the sun. She rolled and she rolled, pointing her toes in the air like a ten-ton ballet dancer, tail whirling – and invariably with the same end result: she fell in the pond with a loud splash. It became quite normal to see Sylvie, looking drenched and a little bewildered, trying to lick her chest as she wandered back down the garden to the house with bits of pond weed and wet leaves clinging to her, and smelling – well, not too brilliant.

WARNINGS AND MISADVENTURES

Over the years Ginge had many misadventures due to his adventurous, daring and active lifestyle. We paid far more in vet's fees for Ginge than any of our other cats put together. Being ginger, he had a certain genetic weakness in relation to his skin, and an allergy to harvest mites – active in the fields in summer – that often caused a lot of problems and irritation. Malc, being far more of a morning person than I am, tended to notice something was wrong well before I did – but he could never actually decide if there *really was* something wrong. One morning he said: "Beloved, do you notice anything funny about Ginge's front paw?" I looked at Ginge through the ghastly blur of 7.30am and saw that his front paw looked as if it had severe elephantiasis.

"Wrong?? WRONG?? It's only swollen to about ten times its normal size!!!" It looked truly ridiculously awful, and in a human would have been incredibly painful, yet Ginge was walking about – jumping even – as if he wasn't in pain at all and hadn't even noticed the *jumbo extension* appended to his leg from the elbow down. Bewildered, we hauled him off to the vet, who decided it was most probably a reaction to a bee-sting and assured us that cats didn't always feel stings as humans do. The paw gradually returned to normal and felt less like a cross between a tree trunk and a sponge.

On another morning Malc said: "Beloved, do you think Ginge is OK?" I slowly fought off the terrible ravages of gravity to look in Ginge's direction. He was moving in total slow motion with a tendency to fall over when he put one paw in front of another. "Oh *****. No. No, he's *definitely not* OK!". It transpired that Ginge had been hit by a car, and was very bruised and had concussion. We had to keep him very quiet and not let him wander around in case he damaged himself further. We took it in turns to sit with the invalid, putting him on a cushion on our laps, trying to allow healing light to pass through us into him and desperately willing him to get well.

We kept him in a soft, closed environment with a litter tray if we had to go out, and carried him into the garden to sit with us in the sun. I don't remember how many days it was before he recovered and was out of danger, but it seemed a terribly long time; we never knew whether he would be fully his active and alert self again, or whether he would be permanently brain-damaged. In the event he made a full recovery and we came to be very glad he had had this narrow escape, as it led him to avoid going anywhere near the road for about the next 10 years.

Another legacy of prowling through long grass on the river bank was Ginge's tendency to get grass seeds in his eye that led to inflammation, and him walking about with one eye shut like a pirate, or bloodshot and weeping. The eye could get quite dangerously swollen and sore without antibiotics, and this was a recurrent ailment. Another frequent need of antibiotics arose from the bites he got in combat with various rodents and other animals. If they went unnoticed beneath his thick fur even the smallest puncture wound could turn into an abcess, and when afflicted by these Pellinore could look a real mess: thus giving rise to some of his less glamorous nick-names – "Old Hole-in-the Head", "Son of Scrofula", "Young Vomit Chops", etc etc. (Though usually, I hasten to point out, if he wasn't called Pellinore or Ginge or Gingeypuss he was called "Beautiful!!" or "Georgeous".)

Due to all the scrapes he got himself in and the need for antibiotics Pellinore was quite used to taking pills. He never ceased to regard them as an unwarranted imposition, however swollen, pustulent or generally dangerous and disgusting his affliction. Usually I held him while Malc got the pill into the mouth. Which was just the start – not, as one might be forgiven for thinking, the end of the matter. Like many cats Ginge learnt to do every variety of convincing gulp and smack of the lips that would convince us the pill was safely on its way, only for us to find him quietly regurgitating it in some out-of-the-way corner a few minutes later. Or worse still, find it, hours later, unobtrusively glued to the surface where we had held him, having been stealthily deposited there minutes after we had praised him for his co-operation, LIBERALLY REWARDED HIM, and set him free. (He nearly always waited until the rewarding snack had been given, and we had exited, before spitting the pill out.)

Children who are abandoned and grow up with animals – whether a pack of urban stray dogs, or animals in the wild, frequently miss all contact with human language at the appropriate "window" for their development. Though hard-wired for language, they also need the experience of it, the contact with it, early in life. If they are introduced to language after that point, so far as I understand, they will never grasp grammar or syntax, just isolated words that denote objects or actions. (Though I wonder if possibly they could, like the great apes, still learn sign language.) I used to think of Ginge as being like a "wild child" in that respect: he could differentiate between words, and recognise what they signified as a dog does, but he was not hard-wired for syntax or an extensive vocabulary.

For about six years before we got Ginge, we had been intermittently caring for Malc's father who had been deprived of the power of speech due to a severe stroke. He could not communicate verbally nor could he write down what he would like to say, although his considerable intellectual powers were almost totally intact. The experience of being with Donald and having to constantly divine what he thought, felt, wanted or didn't want, was a great education. Repeatedly we were brought up against the fact that once the capacity for all language is removed from a human relationship, you are reliant on the kind of signifiers and intuition we normally use to relate to animals in order to communicate with that person. And the person's power to overtly communicate their awareness – and intelligence – is massively diminished.

When we realized how hard it was for Donald to convey his wishes or communicate his own innate and intact intelligence, it further altered our already sympathetic views on animal intelligence. We realized yet more powerfully how easy it is to "project" lack of intelligence and lack of feeling onto animals – and indeed onto people under certain circumstances: as we observed sometimes happening to Donald in hospital with people who didn't know him. I think animals, like human children, may have a "window" where as kittens they can learn to be very attuned to people. Once that window is past, even if they don't become feral, they become less able, more limited in their powers – and need – of interaction. Unlike the other two cats we have now, Ginge – who had come from our friends and neighbours Hugh and Liz and their three near-teenage children – had a great deal of affectionate, understanding contact with people when he was a very young kitten. We found that – as with people – the more we acknowledged Pellinore's intelligence and emotions, the more fruitful and meaningfully interactive the whole relationship became.

On a number of occasions, due to his highly communicative nature, Ginge took it upon himself to draw things to our attention that were potentially either dangerous or disruptive. We came to just accept this as a matter of course. One of the first times was when we were watching television and he came into the room – presumably from having been out – and began to meiow very loudly and insistently at us, and when we looked up, to walk toward the door, stop, turn and meiow again. When we didn't move he came back in the room and repeated his behaviour. Since he was rarely insistent in that way over food, though he might be over an inadvertently locked cat-flap, we eventually got up and followed him. When we reached the kitchen, instead of trotting to the cat-flap, he jumped up beside the kitchen sink and looked at us and then down at the sink – which was overflowing with water where we had left a tap running, so that a large pool was spreading across the floor.

Because we believed in always acknowledging any kind of communicative effort on Ginge's part, we were lavish in our thanks and praise, not to mention plain thankful for having the flood drawn to our attention.

On another occasion – which was rather different – Malc was in his study at the top of the house behind a closed door with another staircase the other side. Pellinore banged the door-handle and meiowed relentlessly until Malc felt impelled to come down, whereupon Pellinore set off scurrying downstairs fast as he could until he came a few feet short of the kitchen door, which was closed. Then he sat down. The see-through glass of the kitchen door was totally opaque: the kitchen was completely full of smoke from a saucepan of food that had been left on the gas ring and forgotten.

Although Ginge's tendency to give us such warnings was not unusual, it was unpredictable, and it was pretty well impossible to know when he would decide (or recognise?) something was amiss: sometimes he just let disasters happen, the way a child might, as if totally unaware of them – or of his capacity to communicate with us.

On another occasion he called us away from the TV late one night, very insistently, into the garden. He walked briskly over the bridge onto the lawn and began to cross it decisively, going toward the end of the garden. He looked back at us over his shoulder every few steps. Eventually, when he had a clear view of our (large) compost-heap about 30 feet away, he sat down and stared at it. We had a torch with us and shone it in the direction he was looking. An *enormous* badger was energetically digging through the big pile of vegetable scraps we had emptied onto the heap earlier that day, old cauliflowers and carrot-ends whizzing through the air with great abandonment to litter the ground around him in a real mess. Pellinore looked up at us and then back at the badger – who, seeing the light of the torch, made a quick, sloping exit into another section of the garden. Ginge just wanted us to know.

CORNWALL

Since we really missed the cats if they were not with us, and used to imagine them saying bitterly as they sat in their pens at the cattery "The *bastards*, the *bastards*", we tended to take them on holiday with us. To begin with (though we got them used to car travel and the cattery as kittens), even on a 5-minute trip to the vet they would meiow in full-scale tragedy-mode to express their displeasure and trauma, and a long journey to Cornwall was a daunting prospect all round.

But pretty soon we cottoned on to the fact that on one journey they would be totally quiet and placid and on another meiow so persistently we had to stop the car – and it seemed to me there must be a reason for the difference. A bit of puzzling and observation revealed that they absolutely hated any kind of *draught*, and that the times when they seemed greatly exercised about not wanting to go somewhere coincided with us having the top or half of a window open, or the fan-heater blowing a discreet blast through the car. Stop the draught and they instantly fell quiet. We felt real heels once we had made the connection, and wondered how many draughty journeys we had unwittingly subjected them to; we took care always to watch the air-streams after that and had very little trouble with them.

Once we reached whatever rented cottage we were staying in and let the cats out of their carriers, they would *surge* through the house, tails in the air, purring, hurrying from room to room to explore thoroughly, jumping onto any low surfaces they found and from there onto the tops of wardrobes, bedside tables, corner shelves etc, knocking over any bedside lamps or ornaments that we had forgotten to secure in time.

In order that we might let them out of the holiday cottages safely into unknown gardens, or to cope with any unforeseen problems on the journey, we bought a couple of rabbit harnesses so we could put them on a lead if necessary. Scarlett (and later Sylvie) took to the harness like a duck to water, and we could stop beside any quiet country field on the journey, put on the lead and lift her out of the car and she would set off like an excited dog, pulling on the lead and eager to explore the new terrain – even having to be forcibly restrained from zooming down rabbit holes in pursuit of Bunnies. As long as we kept her away from the sight of passing cars, she was alert, but fine.

Pellinore, on the other hand, made it quite clear from the word go that he absolutely loathed the harness. There would be a resounding absence of purrs, a stony silence, and he would adopt a stubborn form of passive resistance that Ghandi would have keenly admired. Every paw had to be lifted like a dead weight and squeezed through the soft straps, stiff and sulky.

Every so often he would squirm aside or dodge away to make doing up a buckle more difficult. Once the lead was on, he would crouch down low on the floor with his ears back, a picture of misery.

If we placed him on the ground he would at first refuse to move at all, just sit there crouched and terrifically grumpy. If we gently tugged on the lead or showed him Scarlett walking about happily, he would creep forward as if bowed down by the weight of the world, his belly flattened against the ground, his legs completely bent, moving a bit like a snake. He would go a couple of feet, then crouch down again, stop and refuse to move. If he had not, as soon as we took the harness off, displayed an absolute determination to get out into the cottage gardens, we would have felt it was too cruel to persist; but if the harness was removed he always snapped upright and became determined to get outside, so we felt we had a right to lay down the rules until we were both more familiar with the terrain.

If we picked Ginge up in the harness and stood him in a normal walking posture on his feet, he would simply lie down on his side and refuse to move again. Sometimes he would do this in a completely Laurel & Hardy manner, veering over like a collapsing wall then lying, head on the ground, paws and tail outstretched: over a yard of determinedly passive, short-circuited cat. In the end, it was the time-honoured pathway of *emulating Scarlett* that persuaded him to get on his feet and make the best of things. Scarlett would meanwhile be belting round the garden, sniffing everything, trying to drag us into impossible places, get on shed roofs, attempting to disappear through gaps in fences to meet the neighbours, etc. In the long run Ginge's curiosity would get the better of him and he would – always very cautiously – start to explore. I think because he was always highly territorial himself, he was a great deal more paranoid and anxious when he felt himself to be possibly invading another cat's territory than Scarlett or Sylvie ever were.

Eventually we found a cottage we really loved. It was set in a few acres of private wooded valley with a stream running along beside it and, nearby, an older, derelict cottage with a colony of rare bats inside. There were no other dwellings anywhere near and at intervals during the night tawny owls would sit on the roof hooting to each other, while the stars would burn brightly in the darkness through the trees. There were people-high granite boulders in the surrounding woods, completely covered in mosses, ferns and lichens; and in the morning the sunlight filtered through the young leaves to play on the tangle of collapsing boughs, webs, moths and golden-green rocks. We have returned to this place again and again. Scarlett sadly died before we found it; Pellinore and Sylvie really loved it, though.

As we did not know what creatures might live in the wood or whether Ginge and Sylvie might wander off and get lost, for the first few visits we only let them out with us on leads. Eventually they both became sufficiently secure that they enjoyed going for walks through the trees. We would go out of the cottage and follow a rough path uphill beside the stream through the wood. There were several old, overgrown ruins at the start: the granite, being a paramagnetic rock, encouraged an extraordinary growth of lush vegetation on all its surfaces.

We soon found that a cat on a lead is a very different animal to a dog. They would suddenly decide – all in a moment – that they wanted to climb a tree, and spring from the path up onto a branch, or simply race up the trunk: only to be amazed that they couldn't get further up than about 10 feet because the lead – with us dangling helplessly on the end of it – was holding them back. A battle of wills would ensue, with Ginge or Sylvie determined to get up the tree, and us equally determined not to let go of the lead.

Eventually there would be an undignified backward retreat, with much bad-tempered raking of the tree-trunks, and they would return to the path – only to perversely plunge off straight into a patch of impossible nettles or boggy mud, or up onto a ruined wall and over the other side, with us bent double over the mossy, collapsing stones. They also did not have a dog's conception of "the walk" as a *progression*: an *unfolding route* with a beginning, middle and end. If we came to a gate they would want to jump up onto it and, once ensconced on top of it, would have definite ideas about sitting down, sphinx-like, for a totally unlimited amount of time to survey the view: just like a cat passing the time on a garden wall, or shed roof. So the whole rhythm of these walks was not so much one of *walking*, as sporadic forays of completely unpredictable motivation and direction – and unknown duration. Pellinore particularly liked to take it into his head suddenly to jump across the stream while on the lead, dodge under the barbed wire the other side, wind his lead round as many tree trunks as possible and then *climb a tree on the other side* while we contorted ourselves into a veritable cat's-cradle of arms, legs and leads in our efforts not to strangle him, or be dragged into the water, or cut on the barbed wire.

Eventually when we felt confident that they knew the immediate area, we let them off the leads and just walked through the woods with them, or sat on the grass in front of the house keeping an eye on them as they rambled about. Pellinore would invariably disappear and refuse to come when called, and since Sylvie cannot meiow properly we cannot hear her when she answers us. Once after Sylvie had disappeared and we had been going demented with worry, it transpired she had been parked on top of a high, ancient embankment under a fern, gazing down at us and "quacking" complacently the whole two hours we had been searching.

For the cats, one of the pleasures of being on holiday seemed to be that of uninterrupted access to Malc and I: we had no studies to go to, we were constantly available, and they would make the most of it – frequently competing for the same lap when there were two to choose from, or asserting their right to continuously switch from one of us to the other as often as they pleased. Then they would punctuate the round of attention-seeking with even more stimulating attacks – of attempted armchair-scratching, chasing up and down the stairs, or launching terrible assaults on innocent reclining cushions.

The ultimate treat – as far as the cats were concerned – was being allowed to spend the first night away from home on our bed or beds. This was usually a no-no, as they were both so enormous and heavy: they would lie leaning against our trunks, confining us to an 8" strip at the side of the bed – invariably without any covering left from the duvet. If we pulled on the duvet, anchored as it was by comatose cats, we practically gave ourselves a hernia, and absolutely nothing happened: if you were lucky after five minutes of desperate yanking you would have an extra 1.5" of duvet with which to try and cover your shivering flanks.

If you tried to lift the sleeping Gingeypuss up in order to move the duvet, he was so relaxed and deeply asleep that his body would become like heavily weighted falling silk, sliding inexorably through your grasp to land in a surprised heap back on top of the duvet – and yourself rendered horribly awake by all the effort and deadweight silken limb-juggling. But Sylvie was even worse: if roused from sleep she would be very bad-tempered and not hesitate to defend her bit of duvet absolutely to the death – even if it meant clinging on to a vertically-waving wall of material as you strove to get her off the bed altogether (definitely *without* touching her) in order to redistribute the space more fairly. To say nothing of the 4.00am chases round the bedroom, where jumping on sleeping heads as a *springboard* to the top of a chest-of-drawers was *de rigeur*.

PURRING

Ginge purred the way most beings breathe. You would come into a room and hear purring from behind a curtain – and there was Ginge, sitting in a state of utter contentment gazing out at the world. You would go into the kitchen to grab some coffee between tasks and he would be curled up on "his" kitchen surface, head buried in his tail, a deep, rumbling purr percolating up through the layers of fur. You would look out of the kitchen window into the lean-to greenhouse, and see Ginge stretched out among the pots or couchant in an empty window box, and know, just by glancing at the rhythm of his flanks, that he was pouring out this innate contentment .

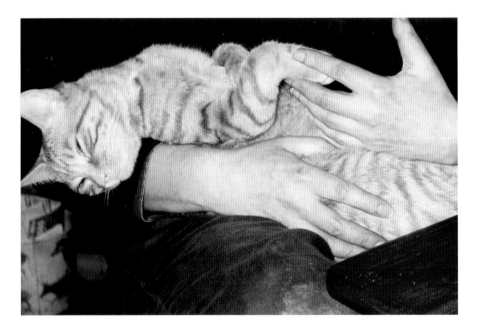

Whether he was roasting himself against a radiator or spending a sub-zero night in the conifer hedge, it was all one to him, all a source of happiness and pleasure. He didn't just purr for England, Ginge purred for the *Universe*. It was such a constant that if Ginge *didn't* purr, we tended to notice, and while taking care not to demand that he purred non-stop, we would pick up on it as an indicator of his mood – the way one would also glance at his face, or gauge his emotions through body-language. He knew we were tuned in to it and he wasn't beyond "the withholding of the purr" as a means of pointing up his displeasure or anger. He was very adept at communicating his moods.

Sometimes when he was curled up, not purring – apparently fast asleep – if you very quietly went over to him and bent down, not touching him: without changing his position at all, without opening his eyes, he would know you were there and quietly start to purr as a way of acknowledging your presence and welcoming you. There were other times when he was quiet, and just sat or lay without purring: often looking as if he was thinking about something or remembering something and was a bit sad, anxious or irritated. If the latter, he was best left alone, and would tend to leave the room if approached. But if he was sad or anxious and you went up and stroked him or picked him up, he would cheer up very quickly and purr in a very warm, fairly quiet way, almost invariably appreciative of the attention.

If you approached him when he was already deep into some arbitrary purring session, as you came up to him the purring would sort of go up a gear: from second into third or fourth, usually with an initial trilling and rising in tone, then settle back into a lower-register cruise-control as you sat down with him or passed on. He was at all times incredibly responsive to the presence of others and quick to demonstrate his pleasure in their company, or to acknowledge their pleasure in his. He seemed to have an innate sense of the value of reciprocation, and the sheer dependability of this boundless inner warmth and spiritual generosity quite obliterated any cynical assumptions regards feline "behavioural motivation".

Purring as a manifestation of happiness or contentment always feels to me to have a very primordial, deep-rooted element. It is as if cats manage never to forget what the safety, warmth, and loving security of very early kittenhood (or even the womb) was like, and they permanently hold this very powerfully positive life-experience inside themselves, as something they can access and re-live when they want to. Whereas it seems we humans lose the memory, and with it the capacity, for such reaching within – or even the capacity for simple happiness – in this deep-seated, restorative way.

If Pellinore was surprised by being stroked, or by a treat, he would also purr with this initial loud trilling noise, quite high-pitched in tone, then as his excitement abated, so the tone of the purr would gradually mellow and fall. If he was just particularly happy – happy to bursting – his purr often took on all kinds of layers of harmonics, seeming to pass through a range of octaves via quarter-tones and obscure sharpened fifths, and was punctuated at intervals by a kind of deep sigh that scattered these smaller, lighter waves of unpredictable purring within its wake.

Pellinore probably purred eighty to ninety percent of the time he wasn't deeply asleep. If he was awake, the odds that he would be purring wherever you came across him – in the snow, in a laundry basket, under a bed – were extremely high. Because of this, he seemed to positively *radiate* happiness, to embody and personify contentment. When we were very low or distressed during the often very difficult years he was with us, he would usually seek us out and come to us bringing the comfort of this enormous power of empathy and affection – always laced with the more down-to-earth animal side of him, that would get bored by too many tears or impatient of too much upheaval, and would express itself in a completely direct, to-the-point way. We regarded him as an excellent, unsentimental role-model.

Though human devotion to animals can drift into folly if we forget to keep our feet on the ground, I think it's true to say that our relationship with animals is often much more simple and pure, less cluttered with ambivalences and ambiguities, than the complexities of (language-steeped) human relationships. It is partly for this reason that animals inspire such abject devotion on our part. We have always felt Pellinore – and Scarlett and Sylvie – are a real inspiration: their profoundly simple, honest, loving spirits show us the way in a world that is all too often a terrible maze of complexity, turmoil and suffering. What they are, and what they express, cuts straight to the soul, and we react to them in a very open, unguarded, deeply emotional way. For this reason it is so devastating when they die: we have no defences built up within the relationship: there is no counter-argument to the torrent of grief.

When he was 14, Pellinore hurt his leg quite badly, and had to be put on anti-inflammatory medicine and kept as still as possible for it to heal. We shut him inside (it was winter) and encouraged him to rest – and so didn't notice, until too late, that all was not well in other ways: he was resting too much, lying about more than he usually would, though purring his heart out as usual. After a brief illness, we very sadly lost him.

When Pellinore died, a great light and a great warmth went out of our lives. I have written this book in the hope of permanently capturing some fleeting remnant of that beautiful radiance.